Technology in Times Past
Ancient Greece

Robert Snedden

A+
Smart Apple Media

Smart Apple Media is published by Black Rabbit Books
P.O. Box 3263, Mankato, Minnesota 56002

Printed in China

Library of Congress Cataloging-in-Publication Data

Snedden, Robert.
    Ancient Greece / Robert Snedden.
    p. cm.—(Smart Apple media—technology in times past)
    Includes index.
    Summary: "Covers the inventions and technology used by Ancient Greeks and how their
ideas influenced technology today"—Provided by publisher.
    ISBN 978-1-59920-296-9
    1. Technology—Greece—History—Juvenile literature. 2. Greece—Civilization—Juvenile
literature. I. Title.
T16.S635 2009
609.38—dc22
                                                                              2007050040

Designed by Helen James
Edited by Pip Morgan
Illustrations by Graham Rosewarne
Picture research by Su Alexander

Picture acknowledgements
Page 7 Wolfgang Kaehler/Corbis; 8 Gianni Dagli Orti/Corbis; 9 Adam Woolfitt/Corbis; 11
National Archaeological Museum Athens/Gianni Dagli Orti/The Art Archive; 12 Musee du
Louvre Paris/Gianni Dagli Orti/The Art Archive; 13 Wolfgang Kaehler/Corbis; 14t Kevin
Schafer/Corbis, b Araldo de Luca/Corbis; 15 Stephanie Maze/Corbis; 16 Peter Connolly/
AKG-Images; 18 Burstein Collection/Corbis; 19t National Archaeological Museum Athens/
Gianni Dagli Orti/The Art Archive, b David Lees/Corbis; 20 Janice Siegel; 21t The Bridgeman
Art Library/Getty Images, b Janice Siegel; 22 Christie's Images/Corbis; 23 Archivo
Iconografico,SA/Corbis; 25 Jonathan Blair/Corbis; 27t Vanni Archive/Corbis, b Art on File/
Corbis; 28 Image courtesy of Tom Malzbender, Hewlett-Packard Company and the
Antikythera Mechanism Research Group; 29 Erich Lessing/AKG-Images; 30 Sandro Vannini/
Corbis; 31 Richard Bryant/Arcaid/Corbis; 32 Alinari Archives/Corbis; 33t Frederic Pitchal/
Sygma/Corbis, b Bettmann/Corbis; 35 John R. Bentley; 36 Mehau Kulyk/Science Photo
Library; 37t Astrid & Hanns-Frieder Michler/Science Photo Library, b Clay Perry/Corbis; 39
Bettmann/Corbis; 40 Time & Life Pictures/Getty Images

Front cover Sandro Vannini/Corbis

9 8 7 6 5 4 3 2 1

CONTENTS

SHAPING OUR WORLD

Our world would probably be a very different place without the influence of ancient Greece. From our alphabet and system of government to our science and mathematics, many of the ideas that we take for granted had their beginnings with the people of Greece.

WORDS AND LETTERS

The alphabet that forms the words you are reading had its origins in the alphabet the Greeks used nearly 3,000 years ago. Many English words, such as history, theater, mechanics, and physics, come from ancient Greek words. When looking for words to describe new ideas (another Greek word), people have often turned to Greek—astronaut, telephone, cinema, and electronics are all formed from Greek words.

THE BEGINNING OF SCIENCE

Ancient Greek thinkers and inventors laid the foundations of modern science. They realized that it was no longer good enough to say the gods caused things to happen. They decided it was time to explain things in a more reasoned way. Scientists such as Aristotle and Archimedes saw how important careful observation and gathering information was in understanding why something happened. The Greeks knew about fossils, for example, and

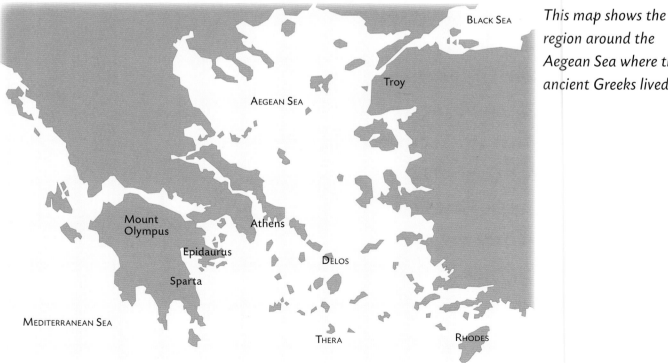

BLACK SEA

Troy

AEGEAN SEA

Mount Olympus

Athens

Epidaurus

DELOS

Sparta

MEDITERRANEAN SEA

THERA

RHODES

This map shows the region around the Aegean Sea where the ancient Greeks lived.

had ideas about extinction and evolution 2,000 years before Charles Darwin came along.

In medicine, too, the Greeks led the way. They studied diseases scientifically, keeping written records of patients and their illnesses. They set out a code of medical ethics that, in revised form, is still sworn to by doctors today.

GREEK TECHNOLOGY

Technology (another Greek word) is the art of producing a useful object from raw materials. The Greeks made many useful things and were competent at metalworking, architecture, shipbuilding, and other activities.

However, the Greeks were not particularly technological because they had slaves to do most of their work and saw no real need to replace them with machines. What the Greeks were really good at was coming up with ideas about how these things actually worked—and

The temples of the Acropolis, including the magnificent Parthenon, have overlooked Athens for more than 2,000 years.

these ideas formed the basis of science. In many ways, the Greeks set the stage for the modern scientific world that we live in today.

DEMOCRACY

Many countries of the world share a system of government called democracy. The word comes from two Greek words: *demos*, which means "people," and *kratos*, which means "to rule." In a democratic country, people have the right to vote for their leaders. The Greeks invented this system in 508 B.C.

HOMES FOR THE GODS

Greek temples were not like churches. They weren't intended to be places where worshippers met but as homes for the gods. The Greeks wanted their gods to feel as comfortable as possible, so the homes they dedicated to them were built on a grand scale.

A temple dedicated to Hephaestus, the Greek god of fire and metalworking, was built with Doric columns.

WORKING IN STONE

The earliest Greek temples were built of wood, but it wasn't long before they were made of longer-lasting stone. Because stone is a much heavier material than wood, the columns supporting the temples were erected closer together to bear the weight of the lintels above them.

The Greeks constructed each column from a number of stones stacked on top of each other, like a pile of coins. The stones were held together with iron rods, just as carpenters use wooden dowels (thick pins of wood) to hold pieces of wood together. Building a temple was a long, hard, and dangerous task. Greek builders erected

COLUMN STYLES

The ancient Greeks developed two main styles of temple architecture: the Doric and the Ionic. The Doric style grew out of the earlier practice of using wood in making columns. Doric buildings were characterized by sturdy columns, each with a plain top, or capital. Buildings in the Ionic style were constructed with slimmer columns standing on a base. Their capitals were decoratively carved with designs such as floral hoops.

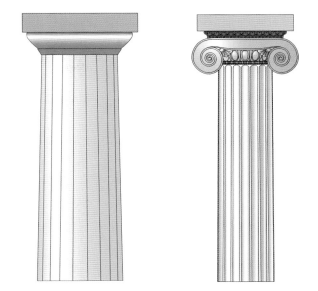

A Doric column (above) has a flat top and vertical parallel grooves. An Ionic column (right) has a decorated top (often with a pair of scrolls) and grooves that are narrower and deeper.

scaffolding and hauled the stone blocks into place using a system of ropes and pulleys. This system of scaffolding and pulleys was the forerunner of the modern crane.

COLONNADES AND COLUMNS

Greek temple builders made some important advances in architecture. One was a row of columns, called the colonnade, surrounding the outside of the temple. Usually, columns supported ceilings or lined open courtyards.

The Greeks cleverly built their columns so they didn't appear to vary in thickness. To do this they used tricks of perspective. For example, the corner columns that could be seen against the sky were made a little thicker and also leaned inward very slightly.

To prevent a column looking thinner toward the top, a bulge was added a third of the way up. Looking up from the ground, the whole column appeared to be the same thickness.

The British Museum in London was designed in the Greek style with Ionic columns.

Building Homes

We can only guess what a typical Greek house looked like. Usually, the houses were made from bricks of mud and straw that were dried in the sun, then laid on a foundation of stones. Mud bricks don't last very long, so there is little left for us to look at today. Often, the mud brick walls were strengthened with timber.

Tiles, Doors, and Windows
The roof of a house had overlapping clay tiles similar to many homes today. The main door was wooden and hung on bronze hinges. Wood was scarce and valuable. If the mud bricks of a house collapsed, the doors were always salvaged and reused in a new house.

Windows on the outside walls were small and set high up, giving the family privacy.

The windows had no glass but could be closed with wooden shutters that were fastened to the walls with bronze hinges.

Around the Courtyard
The rooms of an ordinary Greek house were usually built around a central courtyard. There were bedrooms, a room where the men of the house met their guests, a kitchen where meals were cooked over an open fire,

A typical Greek house (left) had a stone foundation. During the heat of the day, cool air currents circulated through rooms arranged around a central courtyard.

WALL PIERCERS

Mud bricks crumbled very easily and regularly, so homeowners had to make frequent repairs to their property. Burglars were called "wall piercers," because they just broke through the walls of a house to get at any valuables that might be inside.

and places for storage. The furniture was generally wooden. Most often, people sat on stools beside low, three-legged tables that were pushed out of sight beneath couches and beds when they weren't needed.

LIGHT AND WATER

Olive oil lamps made of pottery or bronze provided light. The oil was held in the round body of the lamp with the wick running along the spout. On cold nights, charcoal braziers gave warmth.

Water for the house was carried in jugs from public fountains that were supplied by deep wells. People often bathed sitting upright in a tub of cold water! After, the water was drained from the tubs through clay pipes that led under the floor of the house.

SEWERS AND WASTE

Some city houses were equipped with toilets, flushed out by hand with wastewater and then drained into a sewer under the street. Where there was no toilet, the people of the house had to make do with chamber pots that were emptied into a gutter outside the house or into a pit. In towns, slaves collected the waste and disposed of it in the countryside.

Lamps were made of terra-cotta or bronze and contained olive oil. A cloth wick soaked in the oil burned from the end.

FARMING

Farming was very important in ancient Greece. About four-fifths of the Greek population probably made their living by working on the land. But in the harsh landscape and often dry climate of Greece, farming was not easy.

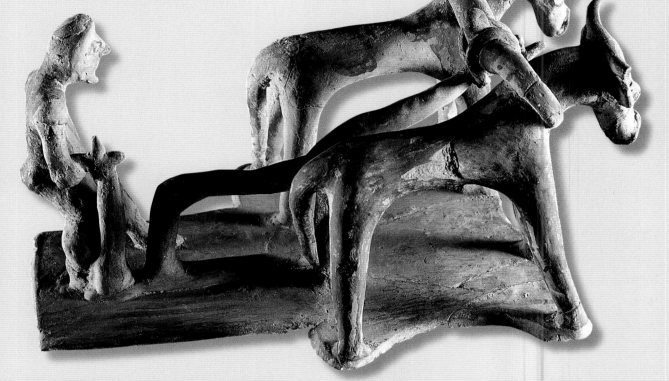

A clay figurine from the seventh century B.C. shows a farmer with his plow and oxen.

GRAIN, GRAPES, AND OLIVES

More than three-fourths of Greece is mountainous, so there is little land for farming. Much of the soil is poor and stony, so land for pastures is hard to find. In addition, very little rain falls between March and October.

The main crops grown by the ancient Greeks were grain, grapes, and olives. Barley, the most common grain crop, was grown on the fertile plains. Grapevines were cultivated on the lower hill slopes, while olives were grown in the poorer soil on higher ground.

PLOWING AND SOWING

Greek farmers plowed their fields at the start of the rainy season in October. Their plows were basic and not very effective. Some plows were no more than a tree sapling with branches pointing in opposite directions. The top branch was used to guide the plow, while the bottom branch was dragged through the soil. The plow was pulled along by a pair of oxen yoked together.

Sometimes the bottom of the plow was covered with bronze, so it went into the ground more easily, but the plowman still had to push down hard as he guided his plow. The Greek plow didn't turn the soil properly and only really scratched the surface. Another man walked behind the plow, scattering seed by hand.

CROP ROTATION

Much of the land was so poor that farmers let a field lie fallow every other year to allow nutrients to return to the soil. Around 400 B.C., the Greeks started crop rotation, planting different crops in the same field.

They followed a three-year cycle: grain one year, a crop of beans the next, then a fallow year. This was a much more productive way to farm. A crop that takes one kind of nutrient from the soil is replaced the next growing season by a different crop that uses different

FARM ANIMALS

Sheep and goats were the most common livestock in ancient Greece because they could survive on poor land that wasn't suitable for dairy cows. Some people kept donkeys and mules as pack animals, while others had an ox or two to help with plowing the soil. Chicken and geese roamed freely around the farmyard and either foraged for themselves or were fed on scraps from the kitchen. Keeping bees was a common practice, and their honey was the only source of sweetness for the Greeks.

nutrients and returns the nutrient the first crop removed. By using crop rotation, fields do not need to lie fallow for so long.

An orchard of olive trees in Greece

BRINGING IN THE HARVEST

A vineyard of grape plants in spring

The ancient Greeks usually stored wine in large clay bottles called amphorae.

Different crops were harvested at different times of the year. Grain crops were sown in October, at the start of the wettest time of the year, and were ready for harvesting in April or May. The grapes were picked in September and the olives in late fall.

SEPARATING THE GRAIN

The grain crops were harvested using metal sickles—the Greeks had no long-handled scythes to make things easier, so harvesting must have been backbreaking work! Once gathered in, the crop was taken for threshing, when the valuable grain was separated from the rest of the plant, called the chaff. The crop was spread out on an area of hard-packed soil, and mules or cattle were driven back and forth over it, their hooves pressing out the grain.

Often, the threshing floors were placed where the wind would blow away the chaff, leaving the heavier grain behind. The farmers helped this separation process by tossing the grain and chaff into the air.

GATHERING OLIVES

Olives were picked by hand or knocked down with sticks. Getting the oil from the olives was hard work. It takes a large number of olives to produce a small quantity of oil. The ripe olives were pressed between two heavy disks of wood or stone on which weights were placed. The oil ran out through grooves in the bottom disk and was collected in clay bottles called amphorae.

MAKING WINE

The Greeks picked grapes by hand, keeping some of the fruit to eat but turning most into wine. They put whole bunches of grapes, including seeds and stems, into big vats. They would stomp on the grapes with bare feet to squeeze out the juice. The juice was left unfiltered to ferment and turn into wine, then it was decanted and stored in clay jars or goatskins. The wine was thick and syrupy, so the Greeks always watered it down before drinking it.

Olive oil was made by crushing olives in a press. Donkeys turned the large stone wheel.

Textiles and Clothing

Ancient Greeks wore tunics or cloaks made from pieces of material that they draped around their shoulders. Cloth was either made at home by Greek women, with the help of household slaves, or bought from the marketplace.

Spinning

Clothes were usually made from sheep's wool or from linen that came from the fibers of the flax plant. Turning wool into cloth involved a number of stages. First, the wool was washed and cleaned, then it was combed to remove tangles. Next, it was spun with a spindle, which was like a stick with a weight, or spindle whorl, at one end. This whorl allowed the user to spin the spindle like a top. The spinner wound the wool onto a long rod, or distaff, and attached one end to the spindle. As the spindle spun, the wool fed onto it and became thread.

Weaving the Thread

The thread was woven into cloth on a loom. The most common loom in ancient Greece

A painting on a vase shows a vertical loom with weights to keep the threads straight.

The man is wrapped in a himation, and the woman wears a chiton.

was the vertical loom. This was either attached to the wall or hung from a ceiling rafter. The weaver attached the vertical warp threads to the top of the frame and used weights below to keep them straight. The weaver then used a shuttle to weave the horizontal weft threads, one at a time, over and under the warp threads.

THE FINISHED CLOTH

The finished cloth was either bleached white or dyed in bright colors. The cloth might be decorated with simple geometric patterns and embroidered borders. The most common garment was the tunic, or chiton. This was made from a big square of cloth pinned at the shoulders and belted around the waist. Women's garments were similar to those worn by men, but were generally longer and more elaborately folded.

THE HIMATION

Both men and women wore a rectangular shaped wrap or cloak, called a himation over the tunic. The himation varied greatly in thickness and size, ranging from something that was more like the light scarves worn by women to a warm, thick cloak for traveling. Men would often simply wrap themselves in a himation rather than wear a tunic.

METALWORKING

Around 1600 to 1100 B.C., the most common metal was bronze. The Greeks started using iron around 1050 B.C., and it became increasingly important. However, they continued to use bronze for many things. Luxury items were made of gold and silver.

WORKING IN BRONZE

Bronze is an alloy, mostly made of copper with a small amount of tin. There is no historical evidence that copper was ever mined on mainland Greece. Metalworkers received most of their supplies of copper from the island of Cyprus. They imported tin from as far away as the mines of Cornwall, England.

This sculpture of a horse is one of many figures and statues the Greeks made from bronze.

The Greeks learned most of their metalworking skills from the Egyptians and mastered a number of methods for working bronze. They hammered it into thin sheets. They shaped and polished it to make household items such as vases and mirrors.

BRONZE STATUES

Bronze was also popular for making statues. Some of these statues were made with the lost wax method. First, the metalworker made a mold from a clay model, then brushed the inside of the mold with melted wax and left it to harden. When it had set, he removed the wax shell from the mold and filled it with a heat-resistant material such as clay. The metalworker attached wax tubes to the outside of the wax shell and made any last minute changes or corrections to the design that were needed.

*A decorated
gold and bronze
dagger blade*

Metal pins hammered through the shell secured it. The metalworker covered it in layers of heat-resistant clay, then put it in an oven. There, the clay dried and the wax ran out through the channels made by the wax tubes. He packed the clay mold in sand, then poured molten bronze through the channels, filling the space left by the wax. When cool, the outer clay and core were removed, revealing the bronze statue.

MAKING IRON

The Greeks only started making iron when they had the technology to produce the high temperatures needed to extract it from iron ore. This involved building a small furnace of brick and lining it with heat-resistant clay. Ironworkers placed layers of iron ore and charcoal in the bottom of the furnace. As the charcoal burned, goatskin bellows kept a constant flow of air into the furnace. This hot exhausting work went on for several hours.

The furnaces could not generate enough heat to create molten metal from the ore, but they did produce a small spongy ball of iron, called a bloom. However, ironworkers had to break open the furnace to get at the iron bloom inside. Then, they hammered the bloom into bars of wrought iron, which were shaped by further heating and hammering.

*This life-size statue of a charioteer holding
reins was erected at Delphi in 474 B.C.*

The Mines of Laurion

The power of Athens, the major city of Greece, was founded on silver. Silver became a major precious metal in the sixth century B.C., and the main supply came from the silver mines at Laurion, about 40 miles (64 km) south of the city.

Slaves in the Shafts

The slaves extracting ore from the mines worked in terrible conditions. Using olive oil lamps for light, the miners dug deep shafts using wrought-iron hammers and chisels, picks, and shovels to follow the veins of silver-bearing ore. They also dug ventilation shafts down into the mine to bring in air.

Thousands of vertical shafts, each a rectangle approximately 3 feet by 6.5 feet (1 x 2 m), were sunk down into the ridges around Laurion. It was a dry area, so there was little risk of flooding. The miners had no wood to prop up the horizontal galleries, so they left pillars of rock to support the tunnel roofs.

Silver from the Rocks

The miners put the silver ore in sacks and carried them up wooden ladders to the surface or hoisted them up with ropes. They crushed the ore with hammers on the hill beside the entrances to the shafts and then washed it.

Silver Coins

The first coins appeared around 650 B.C. in the country of Lydia (in present-day Turkey). These were made of electrum, a natural alloy of gold and silver. The city of Athens used the silver of Laurion to strike one of the world's first all-silver coins in about 580 B.C. The silver brought them great wealth, allowing them to build a strong navy and become a major power in the region.

The owl and olive sprig on this silver coin were sacred to Athena, goddess of wisdom.

They dug great cisterns about 33 feet (10 m) in diameter and lined them with waterproof mortar. These cisterns held water for washing the crushed ore. The miners washed it on sloping marble tables that had grooves to catch the grains of silver ore, while the unwanted rock was washed away. After washing the ore, the used water was collected and recycled back into the cisterns. The ore was fired in small furnaces to extract the metals, which were a mixture of lead and silver. This mixture was then fired again in clay crucibles in a process called cupellation. Some of the lead simply combined with oxygen in the air and escaped as a gas, and some was absorbed into the clay crucible, leaving behind the silver. The silver the Athenians produced was about 98 percent pure.

An entrance (left) to one of the shafts of the silver mines at Laurion.

The remains of a washery (right) at Laurion, where miners washed the silver ore.

THE POTTER'S CRAFT

The Greeks made a variety of clay items for everyday use, ranging from cooking pots, storage jars, and lamps to tiles for their roofs and decorated figure ware. Our word "ceramics" comes from the Greek word *keramos*, which means "potter's clay."

SHAPING THE CLAY

Greek potters often worked together in small workshops that had room for about five or six men. They shaped most of their pots on a potter's wheel made of wood, stone, or fired clay. The wheel was balanced on a pivot and spun by hand. The potter's apprentice often had the job of crouching on the floor and spinning the wheel while the potter worked the clay. Some pots were made by coiling, which meant building up the pot by laying coils of clay on top of each other. Coiled, unglazed pots were used in the home—for example, as storage jars.

After shaping the pot, the potter put it aside to dry. After a time, he smoothed the base of the pot, trimmed off the excess clay, and added handles, which he made separately. The pot was left to dry a little longer before being decorated by a painter. When the decorated pot was completely dry, the potter placed it in a kiln.

The image at the bottom of a drinking cup (top) shows the goddess Athena. The image on the mixing vase (left) shows a scene from a play by the Greek playwright Euripedes.

Figure Ware

Figure ware is a type of pottery made from clay that turned red when it was fired. A painter used black paint prepared from clay, wood ash, and water to decorate a pot with a pattern or figures. He added other details in white and dark red.

When the pot was fired, the potter closed the vents in the kiln, cutting off the supply of oxygen to the inside. The lack of oxygen caused a chemical reaction that turned the whole pot black. Then the potter reopened the vents, which allowed the temperature in the kiln to fall. As a result, the parts of the pot that had been painted black stayed black, but the rest of the pot took on a clear red color.

Firing the Clay

Greek kilns were made from clay and had two chambers—a lower chamber for the fire and an upper chamber to hold the pots. Wood for the fire was pushed in through a low tunnel at the foot of the kiln.

Temperatures inside the kiln could reach more than 1,650°F (899°C). Ancient Greek potters had a number of ways of judging how hot the kiln was. They placed test pieces at the top of the kiln and checked them from time to time to see how the firing was progressing.

The potter also looked into the kiln through a spyhole in the door. His experience allowed him to judge the heat of the kiln from the appearance of the flames.

This container, called a lekythos, was made in the fifth century B.C. for storing olive oil.

TRAVELING BY SHIP

Greece is very mountainous and has many islands, so the best way of traveling from place to place was by sea. There were various kinds of merchant ships for transporting goods and cargoes, and every ship's captain had to be a skilled navigator.

MERCHANT SHIPS

Greek merchant ships sailed over the waters of the Aegean, the Mediterranean, and the Black Sea (an inland sea north of present-day Istanbul). Several ancient shipwrecks have taught us a great deal about Greek merchant vessels and their cargoes. The ships were often built of silver fir, a wood chosen for its lightness and strength. Some were built of cedar wood, imported from Lebanon at the eastern end of the Mediterranean.

A big merchant ship could weigh hundreds of tons, but most Greek ships were small compared with trading ships today. Ships on

A typical Greek merchant ship may have traveled to and from ports throughout the Mediterranean Sea.

short voyages stayed within sight of the coast and probably carried about 30 tons (27 t) of goods. Larger ships sailing across the open sea were able to carry around 90 tons (82 t).

Most ships relied on sail power, but ships called *kerkouroi* were equipped with oars and a ram at the front to fend off the pirate ships that were a constant danger in the Aegean Sea. *Kerkouroi* were often used to carry grain from the Nile in Egypt.

24

FINDING THE WAY

Navigation was very important to the sea captains who wanted to ensure their cargoes arrived at the right place. Those taking the coastal routes from one mainland port to another never lost sight of land. For those traveling between islands, finding the way was a little trickier. They may have followed cloud patterns, because clouds form over land, or they may have detected distinctive smells carried out to sea from an island.

At night, they steered by the stars. Greek sailors knew the heights of certain stars above the horizon at particular times of the year and could use this knowledge to steer. The philosopher Thales of Miletus is said to have taught sailors to navigate by the Little Bear constellation around 600 B.C.

THE ASTROLABE

Greek navigators used an instrument called an astrolabe, or "star grasper." It was based on a star map drawn by the Greek astronomer Hipparchus in the second century B.C. This map was engraved on a disk of brass or bronze 4 to 20 inches (10–51 cm) in diameter. There was a pointer called an alidade at the center. The navigator measured a star's height above the horizon using the pointer and a scale engraved on the back rim of the astrolabe. He figured out the time by comparing the position of the star against the star map on his astrolabe.

A man sails a small replica of the Kyrenia, *an ancient Greek trading vessel found wrecked in the sea near Cyprus. The original was 48.4 feet (14.75 m) long and 11.2 feet (3.4 m) wide.*

TIMEKEEPING

The Egyptians were probably the first to measure time. They knew when to expect the flooding of the Nile each year, and they divided the day into different parts by observing the moving shadows cast by their obelisks. The Greeks adapted some of these ideas and developed them more.

LENGTH OF THE YEAR

The Egyptians had measured the year as 365.25 days long, but the great Greek astronomer Hipparchus was even more accurate. He calculated that the year was slightly shorter, at 365.242 days. This is within about 16 seconds of the most accurate measurement we can make today. Considering he could only view the stars with his naked eyes—without a telescope—this was a truly remarkable achievement.

SUNDIALS

Many ancient Greek sundials were made by cutting a cone shape into a block of stone. The Greek astronomer Aristarchus of Samos is said to have invented the hemispherical sundial, or hemicycle, around 280 B.C.

Instead of a cone shape, Aristarchus created a timekeeping device by cutting a hemisphere out of a cube of stone or wood. He attached a pointer to the block at the center and drew

The pointer on the hemicycle measured the passage of time through the year by marking the changing position of the sun.

a grid on the hemisphere (see above). The tip of the pointer's shadow followed an arc as the sun moved across the sky during the day. The length and position of the arc changed with the seasons as the hours of sunlight increased or decreased and as the position of the sun in the sky changed.

Days and Hours

A different number of arcs were inscribed on the surface of the hemisphere, marking out where the shadow would fall at different times of the year. Each arc was divided equally into 12 so that the time from sunrise to sunset was 12 "hours" long. Because the length of daylight changed as the year progressed, the length of an hour changed, too. Aristarchus's sundial was widely used for many centuries.

The Tower of Winds

The Greeks marked time with horizontal, vertical, and tilted dials. Some Greek sundials were astonishingly complex. The Tower of Winds in Athens, which dates from around 100 B.C., was eight-sided in shape. Each side faced a different point of the compass, and those sides facing the sun had sundials. To help the Athenians tell the time on cloudy days, the tower also contained a water clock called a *clepsydra*.

The eight-sided Tower of Winds in Athens had a sundial on the sides facing the sun.

The Sundial Bridge over the Sacramento River at Turtle Bay in California is aligned exactly north-south.

THE ANTIKYTHERA MECHANISM

In 1900, divers looking for sponges discovered the wreck of a Greek cargo ship that had sunk around 80 B.C., near the tiny island of Antikythera to the northwest of Crete. On board, they found an extraordinary example of ancient technology. In fact, it was so astonishing that for decades no one was quite sure what it actually did.

The Antikythera Mechanism was found in the wreck of a Greek cargo ship.

AN ASTRONOMICAL COMPUTER

The Antikythera Mechanism, as it is known, is a device that seems to act like a mechanical computer, keeping track of the movements of several stars and planets. No other machine as complex as this would be made for more than a thousand years.

The Antikythera Mechanism measures 12.5 by 6 by 4 inches (32 x 16 x 10 cm) and has many bronze gears inside a wooden case with dials on the outside. The ancient device was badly corroded after 2,000 years in the sea, and it took a great deal of effort and ingenuity to reconstruct it.

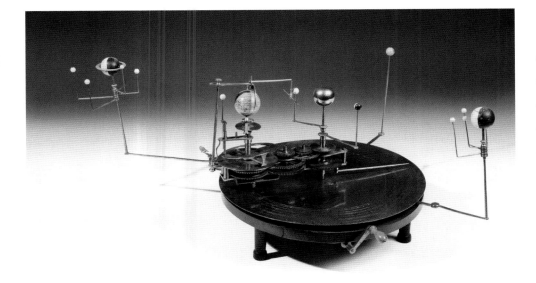

A clockwork device called an orrery is like the Antikythera Mechanism. It was invented in the eighteenth century to describe the motions of the planets around the sun.

THE GREEK UNIVERSE

The Greeks believed that Earth was at the center of the universe and that all other objects in the universe revolved around it on complicated paths called epicycles.

The Antikythera Mechanism copied the motions of the main objects—the sun, moon, and planets of the solar system—as they appeared to move around Earth. Bronze pointers showed the positions of these heavenly bodies on a circular dial that had the constellations of the zodiac around the edge.

The mechanism was like a model of the entire solar system, as it was known to the Greeks. It probably predicted the positions of the heavenly bodies in the sky on any given date.

A CLOCKWORK LEGACY

A smaller device that dates from the sixth century A.D. models the motions of the sun and moon. It provides a link between the Antikythera Mechanism and later Islamic calendar computers. The mechanical knowledge of the Greeks probably passed into the Arab world, then to the skillful clockmakers of Europe and the mechanical toy makers who created automata in the eighteenth century. Modern computers and robots are part of this same tradition.

AN EXPENSIVE TOY?

We can't be certain what the Antikythera Mechanism was used for. Perhaps an astrologer used it as a computer to help draw horoscopes. Or it might simply have been an expensive toy, such as the automata built by Hero of Alexandria. Other such mechanical devices were probably made but have since been lost. Archimedes, for instance, is said to have built at least one orrery.

THEATER TECHNOLOGY

Theater was very important to the Greeks. In fact, they created the first theaters in the Western world. The seats in their huge open-air theaters, called amphitheaters, rose in tiers on three sides of the arena. Most of these held 18,000 people or more.

SOUND MARVELS

The magnificent amphitheater at Epidaurus was built in the fourth century B.C. Members of the audience in the rows farthest from the stage could hear the music and voices from the stage with great clarity. The Greeks had no sound systems to amplify the performance. People wondered if the sounds were carried by the wind blowing from the stage to the audience or if the masks the performers wore acted like megaphones.

In fact, what made it work were the seats. The rows of limestone seats at Epidaurus act like an acoustics filter. They muffle low-frequency background noises such as the sounds of

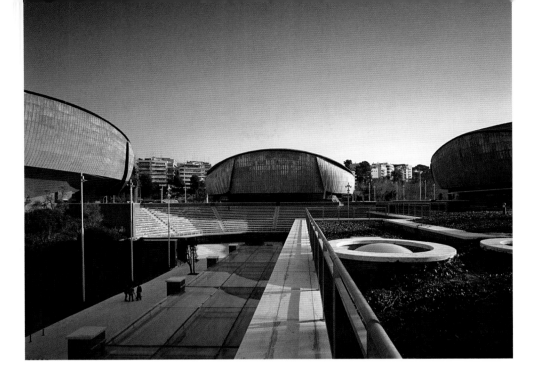

A view of the concert hall at the Parco della Musica from a rooftop garden in Rome.

The ancient amphitheater at Epidaurus (below left) as it is today.

the crowd. The high-frequency noises of the performers on stage are reflected off the seats and back toward the members of the audience sitting opposite. In this way, an actor's voice carried all the way to the farthest rows of the amphitheater.

The Greeks probably did not completely understand how they had made the performances at Epidaurus sound so good. They were never able to duplicate it as well elsewhere and eventually abandoned its design altogether.

MECHANICAL DEVICES

At the back of the stage, the Greeks painted a wooden wall to represent the setting. This was called the *skene*, from which we get our words "scene" and "scenery." Doors in the *skene* could be opened to allow the *ekkyklema*, a sort of platform on wheels, to be rolled out. The idea of the *ekkyklema* was to show action that

had taken place offstage out of sight of the audience—for example, one of the characters being murdered!

Another device was the *mechane*, or "theatrical machine." This was a crane that had a cable with a harness and allowed an actor playing the part of a god to arrive on stage from the air. The *mechane* placed the actor on top of the skene so he could speak to the other human characters from above.

THE GOD FROM THE MACHINE

The Latin phrase *deus ex machina* means "the god from the machine." It refers to an improbable character or event that the author of a book or play introduces to resolve a difficult situation. It was started by some Greek dramatists who introduced a god on a *mechane* at the end of a play to untangle a plot that had gone wrong.

BIRTHPLACE OF SCIENCE

Greek thinkers wanted to find explanations for the way the world worked. They made observations and asked questions about mathematics, astronomy, and biology. The Greeks called these thinkers philosophers, which means "lovers of knowledge," and their work formed the foundations of modern science.

SCIENTIFIC THINKING

Thales of Miletus lived in the sixth century B.C. and is sometimes called the world's first scientist. He is said to have predicted a solar eclipse in 585 B.C. and invented geometry, which he may have used to measure the dimensions of the Egyptian pyramids and calculate the distances of ships from the shore.

Thales started the search for scientific explanations and thought that everything in the natural world could be explained in terms of water as a solid, liquid, or gas. Anaximander, one of his pupils, was quick to disagree. He argued that, since water was wet, how could the dry things in the world be made of it? This was the beginning of scientific thinking and debate: testing an idea by observations of the real world.

THE WORK OF ARISTOTLE

Aristotle (384–322 B.C.) may have had more influence on the development of scientific thinking than anyone else. He believed that technology imitated nature and that much could be learned from observing the natural world carefully. Aristotle produced work that remained unchallenged for many centuries. For example, he described how a chick developed in its egg, how whales and dolphins differed from fish, and how bees organized themselves in their hives. Aristotle

The Greek philosophers Plato and Aristotle are shown debating on this tile from a bell tower in Florence, Italy.

A scientist studies subatomic particles using modern science and technology at a physics laboratory in Geneva, Switzerland.

EARLY EVOLUTION

The philosopher Anaximander had some ideas that were very similar to those of modern scientists. For example, the Greeks knew about fossils, and Anaximander thought that humans had developed from animals—perhaps fish. This idea was an early version of the theory of evolution.

studied the weather and figured out the water cycle, describing how water evaporated from the sea to fall elsewhere as rain.

SCIENCE AND TECHNOLOGY

Today, we think of technology and science as two separate subjects: technology is about making and doing things, while science is about how things work. To the Greeks, all knowledge belonged to one subject—like a spectrum that ranged from knowing how to make bricks of mud to plotting the courses of the planets through the heavens. Practical skills were important. Even the most clever astronomer or physician might design and make his own tools as well as use them.

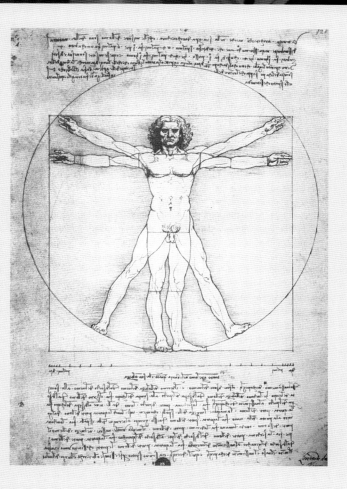

Leonardo da Vinci's fifteenth-century drawing of the human body brings science and art together.

ANCIENT ENGINEERS

The engineers of ancient Greece were very skilled. They invented a number of ingenious devices. Some, such as the water pump, were very useful. Others, such as the "steam sphere" invented by Hero of Alexandria, were less so.

A PULLEY AND A SCREW

Archimedes (ca. 287–ca. 212 B.C.) was one of the world's greatest thinkers and inventors. He was born in Syracuse, Sicily, which is now part of Italy but was then part of Greece.

Archimedes probably invented the compound pulley, which he famously demonstrated by using it to single-handedly haul a ship onto shore. He also invented a device, now called the Archimedes screw (below), for raising water from a lower level to a higher level.

Archimedes is best known for his discovery of the principle of buoyancy. An object placed in a liquid is acted on by an upward force that is equal to the weight of the liquid displaced by the object. Legend says that he realized this in his bath, causing him to leap up and run naked through the streets, shouting "Eureka!" ("I've found it!").

HERO OF ALEXANDRIA

Hero (or Heron) was a Greek inventor who lived in Alexandria, in Egypt, during the first

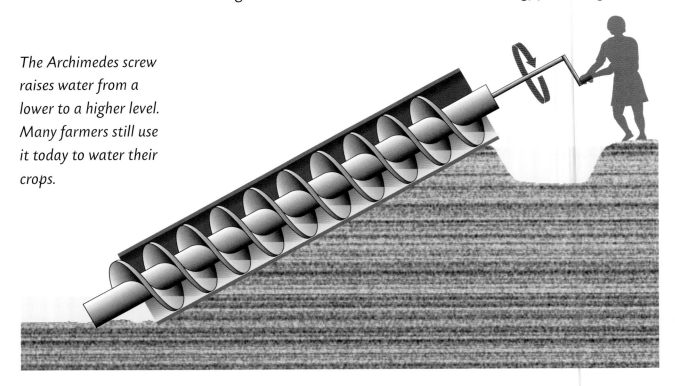

The Archimedes screw raises water from a lower to a higher level. Many farmers still use it today to water their crops.

THE MUSEUM

A temple to the Muses, the Greek goddesses of the arts, was built in Alexandria, Egypt, at the beginning of the third century B.C. This temple was called the Museion—from which we get our word "museum." Copies of every important Greek book were kept here. Engineers and inventors such as Archimedes, Hero, and the astronomer Eratosthenes came to the Museion to discuss their ideas.

sphere and allowed it to turn around. He heated the water in the cauldron from below, filling the sphere with steam. The steam escaped from nozzles on opposite sides, making the sphere spin.

No one ever found a way of harnessing Hero's steam engine, and it was considered a curious toy. Imagine how different the world might have been if the Greeks had discovered the power of steam!

century A.D. Much of what we know about the engineering achievements of the ancient world has come to us through his writing.

Hero invented many things. Among them was the *diopter*, a surveying device that could measure horizontal and vertical angles. It was the forerunner of the theodolite used by surveyors today.

HERO'S STEAM ENGINE

Hero made the first steam engine, which wasn't really an engine at all, but a steam sphere that rotated. It was a sealed, water-filled cauldron with two pipes that held a

A modern model of Hero's steam engine shows the cauldron with the two pipes, the sphere, and the two nozzles.

Greek Medicine

Medicine today owes a lot to the physicians of ancient Greece. Greek doctors followed a high standard of behavior in dealing with their patients, always treating them with respect. They were the first to take a scientific approach to medicine, looking for physical causes of illness, rather than blaming it on the gods and demons.

The Greek warrior Achilles bandages the arm of his friend Patroclus.

In Good Humor

Greek doctors believed that the body contained four substances, or humors: blood, black bile, yellow bile, and phlegm. In a healthy person, these four humors were balanced. People became ill when they had too much or too little of one of these humors.

For example, an excess of blood caused fevers. To treat this, a Greek doctor would let out some of the extra blood by cutting the patient's arm or by applying leeches to consume some of the blood. This treatment was supposed to bring down the patient's fever. It was so common that doctors came to be known as leeches.

Surgeon's Tools

Greek doctors had several surgical instruments to help them treat the sick. Their scalpels looked like those that surgeons use today. They were made of steel, bronze, or a combination of the two, such as a steel blade with a bronze handle. Long scalpels made deep or long cuts, while others, called bellied scalpels, made more delicate and precise cuts.

Greek doctors used two types of hooks: blunt hooks for probing tissues and lifting blood vessels and sharp hooks for removing small pieces of tissue from wounds. Modern surgeons use hooks in much the same way. Bone drills and bone forceps were used to remove bone fragments or weapons that had become embedded in bone. All of these procedures were carried out without the patient receiving an anesthetic.

THE HIPPOCRATIC OATH

Today, medical students take a solemn vow called the Hippocratic Oath, named after the Greek physician Hippocrates who lived in the fourth century B.C. They promise to respect those who have shared their knowledge of medicine and to respect their patients and treat them to the best of their ability.

A medicinal leech can suck a teaspoonful of blood in about 15 minutes.

The leaves of feverfew, an herb with white and yellow flowers, has been used to reduce fever and treat headaches and migraines.

THE DOCTOR'S BAG

A Greek doctor carried a small bronze chest that had separate compartments to hold his equipment—from scalpels and probes to various ointments, drugs, and herbs, such as feverfew. The chest was the ancestor of the doctor's black bag.

MILITARY TECHNOLOGY

The foot soldiers of the Greek army were called hoplites. They were heavily armed with good weapons and armor. Although the hoplites were the main force of the army, they were backed up by a number of cavalrymen, and by some ancient artillery, too.

ARMING THE HOPLITE

All hoplites, whichever city-state they belonged to, were armed in a similar way. They carried large, round shields made of bronze and leather that were big enough to protect them from neck to thigh. A bronze helmet protected the hoplite's head. On his body, he wore a breastplate and a backplate of bronze. Later, these were made of bronze and leather. A hoplite's weapons were a short iron sword and a 6.5-foot (2-m) long, iron-tipped spear.

LAYING SIEGE

In battles between rival Greek city-states, a common tactic was for one side to lay siege to the other side's city. The attacking army took up positions around the defending city and used a number of large weapons to try to defeat it.

The Greeks invented the catapult in the fourth century B.C. The word actually means "shield piercer." The first version was the *gastraphetes*, or "belly bow," which looked like a large crossbow. It took its name from the fact that one end of the weapon rested on the stomach of the person firing it. Later, these weapons became the much bigger *oxybeles*,

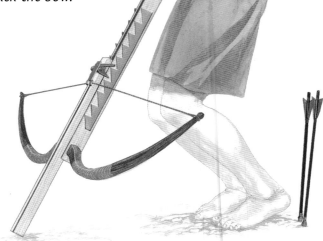

The gastraphetes *had a U-shape on the end where the archer rested his belly while he pulled back the bow.*

or "bow shooters," which were attached to stands with winches for pulling back the bow string.

The heavy artillery came in the form of the *palintonon*, which was basically a giant crossbow. The equivalent piece of equipment in the Roman army was the ballista. The *palintonon* was a weapon that weighed more

A BURNING GLASS

Archimedes is said to have made a "burning glass" that set Roman warships on fire at the siege of Syracuse in 212 B.C. For a long time, people wondered if this could really be true. Then in 2005, a team of engineering students at the Massachusetts Institute of Technology decided to try it. Using a number of mirrors to reflect the rays of the sun, they succeeded in setting a replica ship on fire, showing that Archimedes's burning glass could have worked.

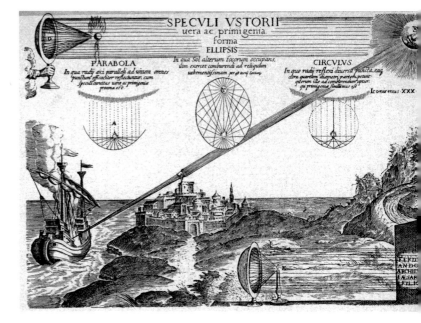

This seventeenth-century illustration by Athanasius Kircher shows the sun's rays and a mirror setting fire to Roman ships at Syracuse.

than 3 tons (2.7 t) and was assembled on the battlefield. Two pieces of rope were pulled back by a winch and twisted to form a powerful spring. They were accurate, powerful, and could fire large stone projectiles at city walls or bolts that could kill several men at once.

The palintonon *could hurl a stone weighing about 9 pounds (4 kg) over a distance of 980 feet (299 m).*

THE GREEK NAVY

Most ancient Greeks lived around the coast of the mainland and on the islands of the Aegean Sea. Ships played a very important part in their lives, not only for transporting goods from place to place but also for defending them from attack and fighting battles against their enemies.

FIGHTING SHIPS

Greek warships had sails like the merchant ships (see page 24), but they also had oarsmen to provide extra speed. One of the earliest Greek warships was the *penteconter*, which had 50 oarsmen. No one is quite sure whether the oarsmen sat in a single row on either side or in two rows on different levels.

THE TRIREME

Around the sixth century B.C., the Greek navy introduced the trireme. This ship had oarsmen sitting three levels above each other on either side of the ship. No one is sure who invented the trireme. It may have been the Greeks or the Phoenicians, who were a great trading nation from the eastern end of the

The oarsmen in a trireme sat in three tiers, one above the other, on either side of the ship. This cross-section shows how the three tiers of oars were probably arranged.

Mediterranean, where Syria and Lebanon are today. They invented the bireme, which had two tiers of oarsmen on either side, during the eighth century B.C.

Greek triremes were probably about 20 feet (6 m) wide and 130 feet (40 m) long. They were fast and maneuverable. Each ship had 174 oarsmen with 13-foot (4 m) long oars and a tall mast made of wood from the spruce tree.

The sailors raised a large sail when the trireme was on the open sea. But when it went into battle, the mast was lowered to the deck to prevent damage. The top speed of a trireme

A British crew mans a modern replica of a trireme near the Island of Poros, Greece.

was probably just over 10 knots, about 11 miles per hour (18 km/h). To keep it fast and light, the trireme carried no supplies. It returned to shore at the end of the day.

INTO BATTLE

The trireme was steered by two large paddles at the stern. Approaching an enemy ship, the oarsmen would row as hard as they could, aiming to hit the enemy ship with the bronze ram at the prow. The whole prow was reinforced to withstand the impact of ramming. Another tactic was to run alongside an enemy ship, breaking off its oars and leaving it immobile and helpless in the water.

For centuries, the trireme was the finest warship in the Aegean and Mediterranean Seas. It was used well into Roman times.

GREEK TIME LINE

ca. 6500 B.C. The first farmers settle in Greece and around the Aegean Sea.

2900 B.C. Metals, particularly bronze and copper, are widely used in Greece.

ca. 2500 B.C. The city of Troy is founded.

ca. 2000 B.C. Sailing ships are used on the Aegean Sea for the first time.

ca. 1900 B.C. The Minoan civilization begins on the island of Crete.

ca. 1600 B.C. The rise of the Mycenaean culture starts in Greece.

ca. 1500 B.C. A massive eruption on the volcanic island of Thera (present-day Santorini) destroys the Minoan civilization. The Mycenaean people take over Crete.

ca. 1250 B.C. Defensive walls are built around many Mycenaean cities. The Trojan War begins.

ca. 1200 B.C. The Mycenaean civilization begins to lose power, probably as a result of famine, and its cities are abandoned.

ca. 1183 B.C. A battle fleet of Mycenaeans is defeated by the Egyptians; the Egyptians call them the "Sea Peoples."

ca. 900 B.C. The city-state of Sparta is founded.

ca. 800 B.C. The Greeks form an alphabet for writing that is the ancestor of the alphabet we use today.

776 B.C. The first Olympic games are held.

750–650 B.C. People from Greece begin to establish colonies in other parts of the Mediterranean.

650 B.C. The first coins are used in Lydia, and in Greece by 600 B.C.

ca. 624–ca. 546 B.C. Thales of Miletus lives.

ca. 530 B.C. The wars with the Persians begin.

508 B.C. A new form of government called democracy is introduced in Athens; this gives all citizens a say in how their city is governed.

ca. 500–ca. 428 B.C. Anaxagoras lives. He is the first person to explain that the light of the sun was reflected by the moon and to describe how a solar eclipse occurs.

479–338 B.C. The great period of Greek classical culture.

ca. 460–ca. 377 B.C. Hippocrates lives. His writings on medicine were the basis of medical practice throughout the ancient world.

490 B.C. The Persians attack the Greek mainland but are defeated at the Battle of Marathon.

480 B.C. Athens is destroyed by the Persians. The Greek navy defeats the Persian navy at the battle of Salamis.

479 B.C. The Persians are driven out of Greece.

431–404 B.C. Peloponnesian War between Athens and Sparta.

384–322 B.C. Aristotle lives. He is a great philosopher and a teacher of Alexander the Great.

338 B.C. King Philip of Macedon takes control of Greece.

310 B.C.–ca. 230 B.C. Aristarchus lives. He is the first person known to have argued that Earth revolved around the sun.

ca. 290 B.C. The great Library of Alexandria, the Museion, is founded.

ca. 287–212 B.C. The great scientist and inventor Archimedes lives.

2nd century B.C. The great astronomer Hipparchus lives.

146 B.C. Greece falls under Roman domination.

ca. 1st century A.D. The engineer and inventor Hero of Alexandria lives.

GLOSSARY

acoustics The science of sound.

alloy A mixture of two or more different metals. Bronze is an alloy of copper and tin.

amphitheater A large outdoor theater with a central round space for the stage and seating that rises on three sides.

anesthetic A type of drug that reduces pain.

astrologer Someone who predicts the future by studying the sun, moon, and planets.

automaton (plural: automata) Mechanical devices that imitate the actions of humans.

bile One of the four humors. Too much bile was said to cause anger and irritability.

bireme An ancient warship with two rows of oarsmen on each side.

bloom A mass of iron formed at the bottom of a furnace.

capital The broader top section of a column.

ceramics Objects made from clay hardened by firing.

chaff Seed coverings and other inedible parts of a plant.

chiton A wool tunic.

cistern An artificial reservoir for storing water.

clepsydra A device for measuring time by the steady flow of water.

colonnade A row of evenly spaced columns supporting a roof.

compound pulley A pulley with several sets of pulley wheels working together.

crucible A vessel that can withstand high temperatures.

cupellation A process for refining silver.

democracy A system of government in which the people elect others to represent them.

dowel A wooden pin used to join two pieces of wood together.

epicycle A small circle whose center moves around the circumference of a larger circle.

ethics Moral principles that affect the way people act.

evolution The process by which living things develop from earlier forms.

fallow A term for farmland that is left for a time without any crops.

gears A series of toothed wheels that are arranged so that one turns another.

hemisphere Half of a sphere.

himation A type of outer garment.

horoscope An astrological forecast of a person's future based on the positions of the planets, moon, and sun at their birth.

mechanics The study of forces and motion.

megaphone A large, funnel-shaped device for making someone's voice sound louder.

navigation The process of planning and following a route from one place to another.

ore A type of rock containing metals.

orrery A clockwork model of the solar system.

phlegm One of the four humors said to be associated with a calm temperament.

pivot A point or shaft around which an object turns.

prow The bow of a ship.

scythe A cutting tool with a long, curved blade at the end of a long pole.

sickle A harvesting tool with a short handle and sharp curved blade.

theodolite An instrument used by surveyors to measure horizontal and vertical angles.

threshing Separating grain from the rest of the plant or the chaff.

trireme An ancient warship with three banks of rowers on each side.

unglazed Without a hard, waterproof coat, or glaze, added to the surface of pottery.

vent An opening through which air flows.

warp The lengthwise threads on a loom.

weft The crosswise threads on a loom that pass over and under the warp threads.

winch A device for lifting or hauling.

FURTHER READING

McGee, Marni. *National Geographic Investigates: Ancient Greece: Archaeology Unlocks the Secrets of Ancient Greece.* Washington, DC: National Geographic, 2007.

Pearson, Anne. *Everyday Life in Ancient Greece.* North Mankato, Minn.: Sea to Sea Publications, 2006.

WEB SITES FOR KIDS

http://www.mrdowling.com/701greece.html
Uncover the "Cradle of Western Civilization" at this site that tells more about the amazing history of ancient Greece.

http://www.arwhead.com/Greeks/
Learn more about the everyday life of the citizens of Athens in ancient Greece.

WEB SITES FOR TEACHERS

http://school.discoveryeducation.com/lessonplans/programs/ancientgreece/
This site provides a helpful lesson plan that focuses on ancient Greek civilization and its influence on the world today.

http://greece.mrdonn.org/lessonplans.html
Find numerous lesson plans and activities on this site that provides a comprehensive overview on ancient Greece, from a lesson plan about ancient money to an activity that brings Greek theater into the classroom.

INDEX